CONTENT

Section 1:
BIBLICAL FOUNDATIONS

WHO IS GOD?

If you are a Christian, it is understood that you believe in God. Naturally, if we are going to study what we believe, we will need to take a close look at who God is and what we believe about Him. So grab your Bible and let's see what we can learn.

1. God is the _____ of the heavens and the earth. (Gen. 1:1)

2. God loves us with an _____ love. (Jer. 31:3)

3. God is _____. (1 Cor. 1:9)

4. God is perfect. He never _____ (Num. 23:19) and he always keeps His _____. (Deut. 7:9)

5. If we confess our sins, God is _____ to _____. (1 John 1:9)

6. God is _____. (Malachi 3:6)

7. God is more _____ than evil. (1 John 4:4)

8. God has a _____. (Jer. 29:11)

Write 1 Timothy 1:17

_____

_____

_____

What has God done for you? Write or draw your answer below.

Additional reading: *Who is God* by John Hay, *The Pursuit of God* by AW Tozer

The second order of business is to make sure that we are getting the right information about God, Jesus, and our faith.

Name some places where you might learn things about God, Jesus, or being a Christian.

_____

_____

You've probably listed some great places like your church, Sunday School, and even your parents. But the most important source is the BIBLE! Often Christians forget to use the Bible to help them know the truth about something. They use the words of people or even something they think they remember. This is very dangerous. Since the Bible says that we are all sinners and likely to make mistakes, we want to rely on a source of truth that does not make mistakes.

2 Peter 1:20 tells us that Scripture does not come from someone's _____.

Whenever we are taught something, we must always be sure it lines up with God's Word and it is not just someone's interpretation.

Read 2 Timothy 3:16. List the 4 things Scripture is to be used for:

1. _____   2. _____

3. _____   4. _____

It's also important that we recognize that the Bible is 100% true- no mistakes.

What I believe about the Bible:

The Word of God is _____. Proverbs 30:5

Jesus quoted the _____ as truth. (Matt. 4:1-11)

Since God does not lie (Heb. 6:18) and can be fully trusted, we have to believe that the Bible is

100% true because 2 Timothy 3:16 says that He _____. it.

Additional Reading: _How Do We Know the Bible is True_ by Ken Ham, _Can I Trust the Bible_ by RC Sproul

WHY AM I HERE?

So now we know who God is and that His Word is the one true source of information. Now what? Well, naturally the next step is to figure out the part we have in all of this.

First let's consider Genesis 1:27. Write it below.

_____

_____

Why did God create us? Well, I think if I were in charge, I would have created what I needed. That's not so with God. He didn't need us (Exodus 3:14). He doesn't need anything. Read Col. 1:16. So why did God create us?

_____. To put it simply, God created us for His pleasure! He enjoys us and enjoys fellowship with us. That's pretty awesome, isn't it?

Read the Westminster Shorter Catechism. Notice question #1 says that our purpose in life is to glorify God and to enjoy Him forever. What do you think that means for your life?

_____

_____

_____

Of course, God's gift of salvation is completely free. He loves us unconditionally, even when we fall short of His desires for our life. But He does have some very specific purposes for our time here on earth and we should know what they are. Read each verse listed below and draw what comes to mind in the space below and to the right.

1.   To know and love God (Mark 12:30)

2.   To be like Christ (Romans 8:29)

3.   To be a part of God's family (Ephesians 1:5)

4.   To serve (Ephesians 2:10)

5.   To share God's love with others (John 17:18 and John 13:34-35)

THE FALL OF PERFECT

We've talked so far about God's incredible love for us, how He takes pleasure in us, and about what He wants us to do here on earth. It all sounds lovely so far, doesn't it? Well, if you've been a Christian for long, you already know that it doesn't all work so perfectly. In fact, the very first people ever created failed, just like you and I.

Read Genesis 3 and summarize it in the box below.

_____

_____

_____

God is always just and He hates sin, which means all people were in huge trouble. Read Proverbs 11:21. Can God ignore sin? _____. Romans 3:23 says that who has sinned? _____. Uh oh. That's you and me, isn't it? What is our punishment?_____ (Romans 6:23).

Oh boy, this isn't good at all. We need someone to save us, don't we? Fortunately, God already knew that and He made a plan all the way back in the Garden. Write below about how God saves us from our sins.

_____

_____

_____

_____

Write (or draw) your personal testimony below.

MY 3 ENEMIES

Although Jesus died to save us from our sin, we now need to be diligent to fight against that sin so it does not become habit in our lives again. To fight any war, we first need to know our enemies. We have 3 very nasty enemies trying to keep us from doing God's will in our lives. Let's take a look at the players.

SATAN

You probably could have guessed that this enemy would be on the list. He's the most well-known for his attempts to cause us to fall. Read 1 Peter 5:8-9. What does it say Satan is trying to do and what can we do about it?

_____

_____

_____

THE FLESH

It's hard to believe sometimes, but our sinful heart is our own worst enemy. Yep, it even beats out Satan. Mark 7:21-23 tells us where our worst sins come from. Draw the answer in the space below.

THE WORLD

Our final enemy is the world. This one is tricky because God tells us to love others. He also tells us to share the Gospel with them. So many Christians blur the lines and become friends with the world. But God gave us very specific commands in His Word about this. Read each passage below and write what it says about the world.

1 John 2:15 _____

1 John 2:16 _____

James 4:4 _____

Galatians 1:4 _____

Additional reading: *Love Not the World* by Randy Leedy

CHRISTIAN LIBERTY

As Christians we have been made free. It's absolutely awesome news, but it's often a very confusing topic. Let's look at some facts.

How were we made free? _____ (Gal. 5:1)

From what have we been made free? _____ (Gal. 2:16)

Jesus died to free us from the obligation that we had to follow the WHOLE law exactly as God had given it. As we mentioned before, the penalty for not keeping every part of the law was death. Aren't you thankful that we are free from that?

But our freedom from this death can be taken advantage of. You see, Christians for centuries have been using these verses to justify (make excuses for) their sinful behavior. Let's make no mistake here. Freedom from the law does not mean freedom to do whatever we want.

Galatians 5:13 says to use liberty NOT as _____ but to

_____.

If we are going to truly serve one another in love, I think we will find that much of the law still very much applies. Remember what Jesus himself said, in Matt. 5:17. Write it here:

_____

_____

_____

As a family, discuss what this "Christian liberty" really means. Write or draw your thoughts below.

Additional reading: _Walking in the Spirit_ by Steve Pettit

DISCERNMENT

So now we come to the part of our Christian walk where we have to make choices about our actions and behaviors as a Christian. This is a really big deal for so many reasons. But first let's remember that we have enemies that do not want us to make good choices.

List those 3 enemies here: _____, _____ and _____

The Bible says that these enemies are very good at tricking us with their lies (John 8:44) so we must be on guard and carefully discern everything we think, hear, or do. Read Phil. 1:9-10 and write it below.

_____

_____

_____

_____

Define discernment using a Bible dictionary:

_____

When we discern whether or not a particular choice is right for our family, we are sometimes called "judgmental." Even other Christians will call us this and remind us that the Bible says not to judge. Well it's true. The Bible tells us not to judge in Matt. 7. Let's look at the meaning of that kind of judge. Click on the link and look under Judge, v. t. just below where is says John 18. Write the definition that #3 gives here (notice that it says Matt. 7 as a reference)

_____

Now let's look at Judge, v. i. just above this. Do you see number 4? It says that the definition for judge is "to discern." In short, discernment is our ability to tell if something is right or wrong. Judging (as used in Matt. 7) is when we determine the punishment for someone else. We are NOT to judge in that way, but we are commanded many times in the Bible to discern right from wrong so that we can make decisions that will helps us please God.

Let's look at a few verses that will be helpful as we make decisions. Make notes on the line.

1 Thess. 5:21 _____

Colossians 2:8 _____

1 Tim. 6:3-5 _____

James 1:5 _____

Hebrews 4:12 _____

Galatians 5:16 _____

Additional reading: _The Law and the Christian_ by Ken Casillas

DISCERNMENT

I have to admit that it's tempting to just try and avoid this whole process. Standing up for our faith is hard. Friends and family might not agree with us. We might even be persecuted for our choices. Do we really have to do this? Read what God tells us to do in Romans 12:2. Then write your answer below using the words from that verse.

_____

_____

_____

_____

One last thought. Often friends or family members may not take the same stand on topics that we do. How will we deal with that? First, 1 Cor. 2:14 reminds us that unsaved people cannot even understand the things of God. So this shouldn't surprise us. We need to keep praying for their salvation, foremost. But let's also remember that the Bible says to love our neighbor. It might not be wise to spend extended amounts of time with someone who doesn't share the same beliefs as us (the Bible cautions us to choose friends wisely), but we can still love them, pray for them, and do our best to point them to the truth.

As a family, make a plan for how you will handle this situation with your family members or close friends.

_____

_____

_____

_____

_____

_____

_____

_____

_____

_____

Additional reading: _The Discipline of Spiritual Discernment_ by Tim Challies

FOUNDATIONS OF FAITH

© Not Consumed 2015

Section 2:
WHAT DO I BELIEVE?

Scripture to study:

Genesis 1
Exodus 20:11
Psalm 90:2
Isaiah 42:5
John 1:1-3
Romans 1:20
Colossians 1:16
Hebrews 1:10
Hebrews 11:3

Additional reading:

The Lie by Ken Ham
The New Answers Book 1 by Ken Ham
Old-Earth Creationism on Trial by Tim Chaffey
One Race One Blood by Ken Ham
Letter to a Theistic Evolutionist by Duane Gish
Scopes Retried by Stephen Bartholomew
The Answers Book for Kids V.1 by Ken Ham

Questions to consider:

Who created the heavens and the earth?
How long did it take (do we believe in 6 literal days, as the Bible says)?
Where did people come from?
What do we believe about evolution?
How can we defend our beliefs?
Are the events in the garden REAL events that actually happened?

CREATION

What we believe about creation _____

_____

_____

_____

_____

_____

_____

_____

_____

_____

_____

_____

_____

_____

_____

_____

_____

_____

_____

_____

_____

_____

_____

_____

_____

_____

_____

Scripture to study:

1 Peter 2:11
Galatians 5:16
Matthew 5:28
1 Corinthians 6:19-20
1 Timothy 2:9
1 Peter 3:3-4
Proverbs 31:30
1 John 2:16
Proverbs 18:22
Hebrews 13:4
James 1:12-15
Matthew 5:8

Additional reading:

The Talk by Luke and Trisha Gilkerson
Teens & Sex by Paul Tripp
God's Design for Sex by Stan Jones
Preparing Your Son For Every Man's Battle by Steven Arterburn
Purity (video series) by Jim Berg
Modesty: More than a Change of Clothes by Martha Peace

Questions to consider:

What does modesty look like in our clothing?
What does purity look like in our lives?
What is considered pornography and how do we protect ourselves?
What is our stance on masturbation?
What level of intimacy should we allow ourselves before marriage?
How do we keep our thought-life pure?
When is makeup ok, if ever?

PURITY

What we believe about purity _____

_____
_____
_____
_____
_____
_____
_____
_____
_____
_____
_____
_____
_____
_____
_____
_____
_____
_____
_____
_____
_____
_____
_____
_____
_____

 MEDIA

Scripture to study:
James 1:12-15
Psalm 101:3
Philippians 4:8
1 Thessalonians 5:22
Romans 12:2
Proverbs 4:23
Galatians 5:19-21
1 Corinthians 13:6
Matthew 6:22-23
Matthew 5:8
Romans 1:29-32
Ephesians 5:19
James 5:13
Psalm 100:1-5
Psalm 119:37

Additional reading:
Tozer on Worship and Entertainment by James Snyder
Harmony at Home by Tim Fisher
Sound Worship by Scott Aniol
The Dark Side of the Internet by Rand Hummel
Upright Downtime by Brian Hand
Amusing Ourselves to Death by Neil Postman
Mommy, Why Can't I Watch That TV Show by Dian Layton

Questions to consider:
Can our hearts and minds remain pure and listen to or watch this?
Where am I putting my priorities as a result of this activity?
What type of music pleases God?
What type of TV pleases God?
What internet activities please God?
What kinds of movies will our family watch and where?

What we believe about media _____

_____

_____

_____

_____

_____

_____

_____

_____

_____

_____

_____

_____

_____

_____

_____

_____

_____

_____

_____

_____

_____

_____

_____

_____

_____

_____

_____

_____

_____

SANCTITY OF MARRIAGE

Scripture to study:
Leviticus 18:22
Romans 1:26-27
1 Corinthians 6:9-10
Hebrews 13:4
Genesis 2:24
Ephesians 5:31-32
Matthew 19:4-6
1 Corinthians 7
Luke 16:18
Proverbs 18:22

Additional reading:
What the Bible Says About Marriage by Ron Moore
Love into Light by Peter Hubbard
The Homosexual Agenda by Alan Sears
Sex Before Marriage: How Far is Too Far by Timothy Lane
An Expose on Teen Sex and Dating by Andy Braner
Sacred Marriage by Gary Thomas

Questions to consider:
What is the biblical definition of marriage?
Is it ok to live together or become intimate before marriage?
Is same-sex marriage ever ok?
How do we handle family members living in marital sin?
What is your position on divorce? Should it ever happen?
What roles do men/women have in the family?
How do you pick a godly spouse?
How do you know when you are ready to marry?

What we believe about the sanctity of marriage _____

_____

_____

_____

_____

_____

_____

_____

_____

_____

_____

_____

_____

_____

_____

_____

_____

_____

_____

_____

_____

_____

_____

_____

_____

_____

Scripture to study:

Jeremiah 1:5
Exodus 20:13
Psalm 127:3
Psalm 139
Genesis 1:27
Genesis 9:6
Job 31:15
Isaiah 49:5
Job 12:10
Isaiah 49:16

Additional reading:

Abortion: A Rational Look at an Emotional Issue by R.C. Sproul
Pro-Life Answers to Pro-Choice Arguments by Randy Alcorn
Birth Control: How Did we Get Here by Kevin Peeples
Does the Birth Control Pill Cause Abortions by Randy Alcorn

Questions to consider:

How does God want us to respond to pregnancy?
Is there ever a time when an abortion is a good choice?
How should we support someone who has had an abortion?
Should we use birth control?
What forms of birth control would be acceptable, if any?
Is there a such thing as too many children?

SANCTITY OF LIFE

What we believe about the sanctity of life _____

_____

_____

_____

_____

_____

_____

_____

_____

_____

_____

_____

_____

_____

_____

_____

_____

_____

_____

_____

_____

_____

_____

_____

_____

OUR CHURCH

Scripture to study:
Hebrews 10:24-25
Colossians 3:16
Acts 2:46-47
Exodus 20:8
Acts 2:42
Hebrews 3:13
1 Corinthians 12:12
Matthew 18:20
Romans 10:17

Additional reading:
Parenting in the Pew by Robbie Castleman
The Glory Due His Name by Gary Reimers
Thoughts on Family Worship by James Alexander
Already Gone by Ken Ham

Questions to consider:
How do we pick a church that is right for our family?
What kind of music, Bibles, and dress code would our church have?
How often do we attend church?
Do we attend Sunday School?
How do we behave in the services? Is coloring/drawing allowed?
Do we attend children's church? Until how long?
How involved is our family in service at church?
What issues should we refuse to compromise on?
What part does church play in our daily lives?

What we believe about our church _____

_____

_____

_____

_____

_____

_____

_____

_____

_____

_____

_____

_____

_____

_____

_____

_____

_____

_____

_____

_____

_____

_____

_____

_____

_____

_____

_____

# ALCOHOL

Scripture to study:
Ephesians 5:18
Proverbs 20:1
Proverbs 23:29-35
Isaiah 5:11
Galatians 5:21
Romans 13:13
1 Corinthians 6:19-20
1 Corinthians 3:16-17
1 Peter 5:8
1 Peter 4:7

Additional reading:
Christians and Alcohol by Randy Jaeggli
Alcohol Today: Abstinence in the Age of Indulgence by Peter Lumpkins
Talking to Your Kids about Drugs and Alcohol by James Dobson

Questions to consider:
What is our position on drinking?
What does the Bible say about being drunk? How will we respond?
If we drink alcohol can we truly be filled with the Spirit?
Are we willing to put substances in our bodies that inhibit our thinking? Should we be?
How might our position on drinking affect a fellow believer?
Is alcohol harmful to the body?
Are cigarettes and drugs harmful to the body?
What will we do if faced with one of these substances?
How can mom/dad help if the situation gets out of control?

ALCOHOL

What we believe about alcohol _____

_____

_____

_____

_____

_____

_____

_____

_____

_____

_____

_____

_____

_____

_____

_____

_____

_____

_____

_____

_____

_____

_____

_____

_____

_____

_____

Scripture to study:

2 Corinthians 9:7
Acts 20:35
Luke 6:38
Proverbs 3:27
Proverbs 19:17
Matthew 6:19-21
Proverbs 22:7
Luke 14:28
Matthew 6:33
Proverbs 3:9-10
Romans 13:8
Proverbs 13:22

Additional reading:

The Treasure Principle by Randy Alcorn
The Legacy Journey by Dave Ramsey
Smart Money, Smart Kids by Dave Ramsey

Questions to consider:

What is good stewardship?
How much do we give to the local church?
How much do we give to missions?
How much are we saving?
How are we building good habits with our finances?
Are there things that we can't support financially?
How much are we giving to others?

MONEY

What we believe about money _____

_____

_____

_____

_____

_____

_____

_____

_____

_____

_____

_____

_____

_____

_____

_____

_____

_____

_____

_____

_____

_____

_____

_____

_____

_____

_____

# HOLIDAYS

Scripture to study:
Jeremiah 10:1-4
Deuteronomy 12:29-32
Matthew 15:3
Romans 12:1-3
Philippians 2:15
Colossians 2:8

Additional reading:
The Christ of Christmas by James Boice
The War on Christmas by Bodie Hodge
Mommy, Why Don't We Celebrate Halloween? by Linda Winwood
Halloween History and the Bible by Bodie Hodge
In Defense of Easter by Tim Chaffey
Are the Symbols and Customs of Easter of Pagan Origin by Roger Patterson

Questions to consider:
What holidays do our family consider to be important to our faith?
How do we protect our faith from worldly activities during those holidays?
Which holidays do we abstain from and why?
Are Santa, the Easter Bunny, and the Tooth Fairy a part of our traditions?
Does this holiday promote false doctrine or immorality?
Can we participate in this holiday while giving thanks and praise to God?
Will the holiday detract from our witness?

HOLIDAYS

What we believe about holidays _____

_____

_____

_____

_____

_____

_____

_____

_____

_____

_____

_____

_____

_____

_____

_____

_____

_____

_____

_____

_____

_____

_____

_____

_____

Section 3:
BONUSES

MEDIA CHECKLIST

MOVIE TITLE

RATING	☆ ☆ ☆ ☆ ☆	DATE

What is the underlying message of the movie?

_____

_____

_____

Does this message contradict God's word?
☐ YES ☐ NO

Are the characters people who would be godly examples for us?
☐ YES ☐ NO

Is the music in the movie offensive to God?
☐ YES ☐ NO

Would I be embarrassed if someone saw me watching it?
☐ YES ☐ NO

Does the movie portray sin as good or exonerate it?

THIS MOVIE IS ☐ Lovely

☐ Honorable ☐ Commendable

☐ Just ☐ Excellent

☐ Pure ☐ Worthy of Praise

My purpose in life

TO KNOW & L♥VE GOD
MARK 12:30

to be like Christ
ROMANS 8:29

TO SHARE GOD'S love with each other
JOHN 17:18

to be a part of GOD'S FAMILY
EPHESIANS ONE:FIVE

to SERVE
EPH 2:10

Keep your heart with all vigilance, for from it flow THE SPRINGS OF LIFE
Proverbs 4:23

Keep your heart with all vigilance, for from it flow THE SPRINGS OF LIFE
Proverbs 4:23

Keep your heart with all vigilance, for from it flow THE SPRINGS OF LIFE
Proverbs 4:23

Keep your heart with all vigilance, for from it flow THE SPRINGS OF LIFE
Proverbs 4:23

Keep your heart with all vigilance, for from it flow THE SPRINGS OF LIFE
Proverbs 4:23

Keep your heart with all vigilance, for from it flow THE SPRINGS OF LIFE
Proverbs 4:23

Keep your heart with all vigilance, for from it flow THE SPRINGS OF LIFE
Proverbs 4:23

Keep your heart with all vigilance, for from it flow THE SPRINGS OF LIFE
Proverbs 4:23

Keep your heart with all vigilance, for from it flow THE SPRINGS OF LIFE
Proverbs 4:23

Keep your heart with all vigilance, for from it flow THE SPRINGS OF LIFE
Proverbs 4:23

Made in the USA
Middletown, DE
17 March 2017